**Animal Peculiarity Volume 2 Part 1**

*By T.P Just*

~~~

I0439293

**Get All The Books In The Series:**

Animal Peculiarity Volume 1 [1-8]
Animal Peculiarity Volume 2 [1-8]
**Just Enterprises**

# Table of Contents

# 1 Introduction

Suicide is commended as an escape from the ills of life, and riches are to be despised. Aelian's Stoicism hardly goes below the surface. His primary object is to entertain and while so doing to convey instruction in the most agreeable form.

He was among the first to break away from the age-long tradition of the periodic structure of sentences, at least for works of a serious nature, and to affect a simpler prose of short, coordinated, sometimes paratactic, clauses.

In this and in the rich variety of topics and in a certain fondness for piquant, not to say earthy, stories from the life of men and of animals one may trace the influence of the Milesian Tales. Unfettered by any canons of style or language, picaresque, and sometimes gross, they pandered to popular taste.

To adopt their technique while refining the style and imparting a moral flavour to his narratives may well have seemed to Aelian a sure way of gaining a like popularity with educated readers. Some might find fault with his random and piece-meal handling of his theme-of that he is well aware, and in the Epilogue he defends himself with the plea that a frequent change of topic helps to maintain the reader's interest and saves him from boredom,

But as to the permanent value of his work he has no misgivings, and since, Philostratus informs us that his writings were much admired, we may assume that they appealed to cultivated circles in a way that the voluminous and possibly arid compilations of grammarians did not.

The knowledge which Aelian displays of Egypt and its topography, its local traditions, customs, and religious beliefs, especially those relating to birds and animals can come only from a writer well acquainted with the land and its people.

We are given mystical and mythological reasons for the reverence or detestation in which certain creatures are held, there are tales of wonder ranging from the merely curious to the impossible; quotations from Homer are introduced into chapters on Egyptian religion.

The pattern fits Apion (1st cent. A.D.). Born in the Great Oasis, he became head of the Alexandrian school, was a Homeric scholar and a pretender to omniscience.

His Aegyptiaca was a compilation dealing with the history and the marvels of Egypt and was based upon earlier writers with additions from his own experience. One such there is which 'every schoolboy knows,' the story of Androcles and the Lion.

In determining the modern equivalents and the scientific nomenclature of the fauna and flora of Ancient Greece the oracles do not always speak with one voice, and the best that a layman can hope for is that, when two or more interpretations have presented themselves, the result of his choice may be judged, if not correct, at any rate excusable.

# 2 The Partridge

You would never hear the same note from all Partridges, but
they vary. At Athens for instance those on the far side of the
deme Corydallus emit one note, those on this side another.
What names these notes have Theophrastus will tell us. But in
Boeotia and on the opposite shore of Euboea they have the
same note and, as it were, the same language. In Cyrene the
Frogs are completely dumb; in Macedonia, the Pigs; and there
is also a kind of Cicada that is dumb.

# 3 The Grape-spider

There is a kind of Spider which they call the 'Grape-spider,' either because it is dark and does in fact resemble a grape in a bunch-it has a somewhat spherical appearance-or for some other reason.

It occurs in Libya and has short legs; it has a mouth in the middle of its belly, and can kill in a twinkling.

# 4 The Frogs of Seriphus

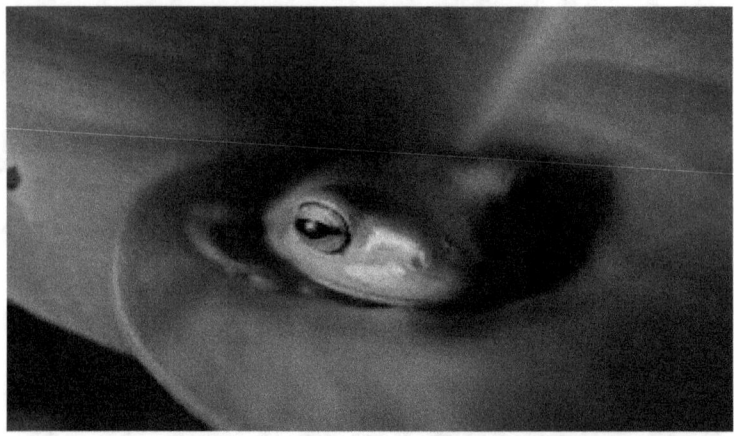

In Seriphus you will never hear the Frogs croaking at all. If however you transport them elsewhere, they emit a piercing and most harsh sound.

On mount Pierus in Thessaly there is a lake; it is not perennial but is created in winter by the waters which flow together into it.

**And Perseus**

Now if one throws Frogs into it they become silent, though vocal elsewhere. Touching the Seriphian Frogs the people of Seriphus boast that Perseus arrived from his contest with the and Perseus Gorgon after covering an immense distance, and being naturally fatigued rested by the lake side and lay down wishing to sleep. The Frogs however worried the hero with their croaking and interrupted his slumbers.

But Perseus prayed to his father to silence the Frogs. His father gave ear and to gratify his son condemned the Frogs there to everlasting silence. Theophrastus however upsets the story and relieves the Seriphians of their imposture by asserting that it is the coldness of the water that causes the aforesaid Frogs to be dumb.

## Local Peculiarities

In moist places and where the air is excessively damp Cocks do not crow, according to Theophrastus and the lake at Pheneus produces no fish. It is because Cicadas are constitutionally cold that, when warmed by the sun, they sing, says the same writer.

# 5 The Goat-Sucker

It seems that the Goatsucker is the most audacious of creatures, for it despises small birds but suck assails goats with the utmost violence, and more than that, it flies to their udders and sucks out the milk without any fear of vengeance from the goatherd, although it makes the basest return for being filled with milk, for it makes the dug 'blind' and staunches its flow.

# 6 The Nightingale

Many people sing the praises of the son of Arete, the sister "of Aristippus, as being taught by his mother. Aristotle says that he has with his own eyes seen the young of the Nightingale being instructed by their mother how to sing.

It seems that the Nightingale passionately loves its freedom, and for that reason when a mature bird is caught and confined in a cage, it refrains from song and takes vengeance on the birdwatcher for its enslavement by silence. Consequently men who have had this experience let them go when they are older and do their best to catch the young.

### The Horn of the unicorn

India produces horses with one horn, they say, and the same country fosters asses with a single horn. And from these horns they make drinking vessels, and if anyone puts a deadly poison in them and a man drinks, the plot will do him no harm. For it seems that the horn both of the horse and of the ass is an antidote to the poison.

# 7 The Peacock

The Peacock on the contrary, which is a beautiful bird, is
killed and eaten by voluptuaries. The feathers of this bird are
a decoration, though its body is of little or no account.
But I never heard of anyone killing a Purple Coot for a meal,
not Callias nor Ctesippus the Athenians, not Lucullus nor
Hortensius the Romans. I have named but a few out of many
who were luxurious and in satiate in other ways but especially
where their bellies were concerned.

## The Purple Coot

The Purple Coot is the most beautiful and the most
appropriately named of creatures, and it de- lights to dust
itself, and it also bathes just as pigeons do.
But it does not devote itself to the dusting- place or to the bath
until it has walked a certain number of paces to satisfy itself. It
cannot bear being seen feeding, and for that reason it retires
and eats in concealment.

It is violent in its jealousy and keeps a close watch on the mated female birds, and if it discovers the mistress of its house to be adulterous, it strangles itself. It does not fly high. Yet men take pleasure in it and tend it with care and consideration.

And apparently it is either a pet in a. sumptuous and opulent household, or else it is admitted into a temple and roams unconfined, moving about as a sacred creature within the precinct.

# 8 The Raven in old age

When the Raven on reaching old age can no longer feed its young, it offers itself as their food; and they eat their father. And this is alleged to be the origin of the proverb which says 'A bad egg of a bad raven.'

## The Ringdove

Ringdoves are celebrated as the most continent of birds. For instance, when once the male and the female have paired and are, so to say, of one mind to Wed, they cling to one another and are continent, and neither bird would touch a strange bed. If however they cast amorous glances at other birds, the rest gather round them and the male is torn to pieces by those of his own sex, the female by the females.

This then is the law of continence which extends to doves and remains unchanged, except that they do not put to death both birds: when they kill the male they take compassion on the female and leave her unharmed ; and she goes about, a widow.

## The Pigeon

Aristotle says that male Pigeons share the birth-pangs of the females, and if they wander from the nest the males will push and drive them in; and when they have laid their "eggs the males will force them to brood them.

But the male birds also keep the chicks Warm and help the females to feed them, according to the same writer. And to prevent the chicks from being underfed the parents begin by giving them saline earth, so that when they have tasted it, they then readily eat the -rest of their food.

It would seem that there is a treaty of peace between Pigeons and such others as are birds of prey, but they are said to live in fear of sea-eagles and falcons. But their method of dealing with hawks is a tale worth hearing.

### And Hawks

When the hawk, which is accustomed to soar high in the air, gives chase, the Pigeons glide and sink lower and attempt to reduce their flight.

When attacked however by some bird which by nature flies at a lower level than they, the Pigeons mount up and travel through the sky, and flying overhead they have no fear, because the other cannot harry them from above.

# 9 A white Elephant

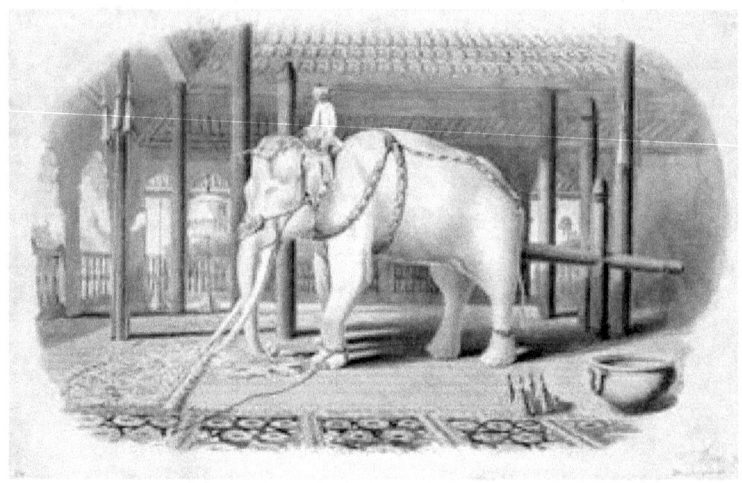

An Indian trainer finding a young white Elephant took and reared it during its early years; he gradually tamed it and used to ride upon it and grew fond of his chattel, which returned his affection and recompensed him for his fostering care.

Now the king of the Indies hearing of this, asked to be given the animal. But the trainer in his affection was jealous and even overcome with grief at the thought of another man being its master, and declined to give it up; and so, mounting the Elephant, he went off into the desert.

The king in his indignation dispatched men to take the Elephant away and at the same time to bring the Indian to judgment. When they arrived they attempted to apply force. So the man struck at them from his mount, and the beast helped to defend its master as he was being injured.

Such was the beginning of the affair. But when the Indian was wounded and fell, the Elephant bestrode its keeper after the manner of armed men covering a comrade with their shields, slew many of the attackers, and put the remainder to flight.

Then, winding its trunk round its keeper, it raised him and brought him to its stable and stayed by his side, as one trusty friend might do to another, thus showing its kindly nature. O wicked men, forever busy about the table and the clash of frying-pans and dancing to your lunch, but traitors in the hour of danger, in whose mouth the word 'Friendship' is vain and of no effect.

# 10 Examples of incest

In the name of Zeus our father, permit me to ask the tragic dramatists and their predecessors, the inventors of fables, what they mean by showering such a flood of ignorance upon the son of Laius who consummated that disastrous union with his mother; and upon Telephus who, without indeed attempting union, lay with his mother and would a have done the same as Oedipus, had not a serpent sent by the gods kept them apart, when Nature allows unreasoning animals to perceive by mere contact the nature of this union, with no need for tokens nor for the presence of the man who exposed Oedipus on Cithaeron.

The Camel, for instance, would never couple with its mother. Now the keeper of a herd of camels covered up a female as far as possible, hiding all but its parts, and then drove the son to its mother. The beast, all unwitting, in its eagerness to copulate, did the deed, and then realised what it had done. It bit and trampled on the man who was the cause of its unlawful union, and kneeling on him put him to an agonizing death, and then threw itself over a precipice.

And here Oedipus was ill-advised in not killing himself but blinding his eyes; in not realising how to escape from his calamities when he might have made away with himself instead of cursing his house and his family; and finally in seeking by an irremediable calamity to remedy calamities already past.

# 11 The Partridge

Partridges are the most incontinent of birds; that is the reason for their passionate love of the female birds and for their constant enslavement to lust. So those that rear fighting Partridges, when they egg them on to battle with one another, make the female stand each by her mate, as they have found this to be a device for countering any cowardice or reluctance to fight.

For the Partridge that is defeated cannot endure to show himself either to his loved one or to his spouse. He will sooner die under the blows than turn away from his adversary and dare in his disgrace to look upon her whose good opinion he courts.

# 12 Cretan lovers

The Cretans also have taken this view regarding lovers. For I have heard that a Cretan lover, who had beside other qualities that of a fine soldier, had as his favourite a boy of good birth, conspicuous for his beauty, of manly spirit, excellently fitted by nature to imbibe the noblest principles, though on account of his youth he was not yet called to arms.

(I have elsewhere given the name of the lover and of the beautiful boy.) Now the Cretans say that the young man did acts of valour in the fight, but when the enemy's massed line pressed him hard, he stumbled over a dead body that lay there and was thrown down.

Whereupon one of the enemy who was nearest, in his eagerness was about to strike him in the back. But the man turned and exclaimed ' Do not deal me a shameful and cowardly blow, but strike me in front, in the breast, in order that my loved one may not judge me guilty of cowardice and refrain from laying out my dead body ,he could not bear to go near one who so disgraces himself.

There is nothing wonderful in a man being ashamed to appear a coward, but that a Partridge should have some feeling of shame, this is a truly impressive gift of Nature. But Aristodemus the timid, and Cleonymus who threw away his shield, and Pisander the craven, had no reverence for their country or for their wives or for their children.

# 13 The Pigeons of Aphrodite at Eyrx

At Eryx in Sicily there is a festival which not only the people of Eryx but everybody throughout the whole of Sicily as well call the 'Festival of the Embarkation.' And the reason why the festival is so called is this: they say that during these days Aphrodite sets out thence for Libya.

They adduce in support of their belief the following circumstance. There is there an immense multitude of Pigeons. Now these disappear, and the people of Eryx assert that they have gone as an escort to the goddess, for they speak of Pigeons as 'pets of Aphrodite,' and so everybody believes them to be.

But after nine 'days one bird of conspicuous beauty is seen flying in from the sea which brings it from Libya: it is not like the other Pigeons in a flock but is rose-coloured, just as Anacreon of Teos describes Aphrodite, styling her somewhere 'roseate'. And the bird might also be compared to gold, for this too is like the same goddess of whom Homer sings as 'golden '

And after the bird follow the other Pigeons in clouds, and again there is a festal gathering for the people of Eryx, the 'Festival of the Return '; the name is derived from the event.

# 14 Lion and Lioness

The Wolf and the she-Wolf feed together, like- wise the Horse and- the Mare; the Lion and the Lioness however do not, for the Lioness and the Lion do not follow the same track either hunting or when drinking.
And the reason is that both derive confidence from their bodily strength, so that neither has need of the other, as older writers assert.

### The Wolf

Wolves are not easily delivered of their young; only after twelve days and twelve nights, for the people of Delos maintain that this was the length of time that it took Leto to travel from the Hyperborean's to Delos.

### Animal enmities

Animals hostile to one another: the Tortoise and the Partridge; the Stork and the Corncrake, to the Sea-gull; the Shearwater and the Heron to the Sea-mew;

The Crested Lark feels enmity towards the Goldfinch; the Turtle-dove disagrees with the Pyrallis; the Kite too and the Raven are enemies; the Siren and the Circe; the Circe and the Falcon have been found to be at variance not only in the matter of sex but in their nature.

# 15 The Horse

Men skilled in the breeding and care of Horses agree that Horses are most fond of marshy ground, meadows, and wind-swept spots. Hence we find Homer, who in my opinion had a remarkable know- ledge of such matters, saying somewhere, 'For him three thousand mares grazed along the water—meadow.'

### Mares impregnated by the wind

And horse-keepers frequently testify to Mares being impregnated by the wind, and to their galloping against the south or the north wind. And the same poet knew this when he said, 'Of them was Boreas enamoured as they pastured'. Aristotle too, borrowing (as I think) from him, said that they rush away in frenzy straight in the face of the aforesaid winds.

# 16 Example of animal incest

I am told that the King of the Scythians (his name I know but suppress, for I have nothing to gain by it) possessed a mare remarkable for every excellence which is expected of horses and for which they are displayed; and that he possessed also a foal of this same mare which surpassed all others in its excellence.

Being unable to find either another worthy mate for the mare or another mare fit to be impregnated by the foal, he therefore put the two together for that purpose. They caressed each other in various ways and were friendly disposed, but refused to couple.

So as the animals were too clever for the Scythians' scheme, he blindfolded both mare and foal with cloths, and they accomplished the act so contrary to law and morality. But when the pair realised what they had done, they atoned for their impious deed by death and threw themselves over a precipice.

# 17 Fish in the mating season

The majorities of Fishes are eager for sexual intercourse throughout the springtime, and withdraw for choice to the Black Sea, for it contains caverns and resting-places which are Nature's gift to Fishes.

Besides, its waters are free from the savage creatures which the sea breeds. Only dolphins roam there, and they are small and feeble. Moreover it is devoid of octopuses; it produces no crabs and does not breed lobsters: these are the bane of small fishes

**Get All The Books In The Series:**

Animal Peculiarity Volume 1 [1-8]
Animal Peculiarity Volume 2 [1-8]

www.ingramcontent.com/pod-product-compliance
Lightning Source LLC
Chambersburg PA
CBHW060351290526
45791CB00004B/1631